LOWELL HOUSE JUVENILE

GRUESOME GRUB
AND
DISGUSTING DISHES

Susan Martineau
Illustrations by Martin Ursell
With thanks for the idea to Marta Fumagalli

First published in Great Britain by b small publishing,
Pinewood, 3a Coombe Ridings, Kingston upon Thames, Surrey KT2 7JT
© b small publishing 1999
American edition published in 2000 by Lowell House
A division of NTC/Contemporary Publishing Group, Inc.
4255 West Touhy Avenue, Lincolnwood (Chicago), Illinois 60712 U.S.A.

Color reproduction: Vimnice International Ltd., Hong Kong. Printed in Hong Kong by Wing King Tong Co. Ltd.
Editorial: Catherine Bruzzone and Susan Martineau   *Design*: Lone Morton   *Production*: Grahame Griffiths

Library of Congress Catalog Card Number: 99-85872
ISBN: 0-7373-0428-6
10 9 8 7 6 5 4 3 2 1

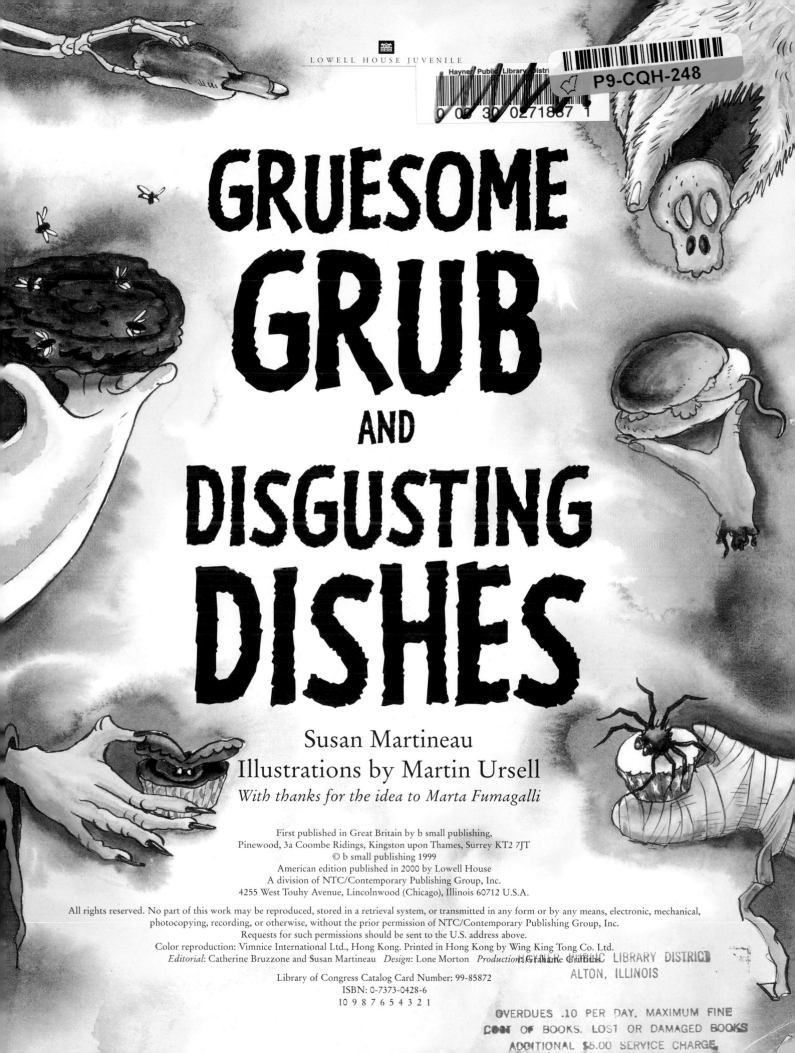

Before You Begin

To get the best results from your gruesome cooking, here are a few tips:

Once you've chosen a recipe, it's a good idea to read it all the way through and get all your equipment and ingredients ready before you start. The recipes list exactly what you will need.

You should always have a grownup standing by to help with any recipe steps requiring you to heat food or use a sharp knife.

Keep some oven mitts handy for recipes involving hot food.

Always wash your hands and put on an apron before cooking. Make sure your work surfaces are nice and clean.

Afterward…don't forget to clean up!

Unless otherwise noted, all the recipes serve 4 people.

All the spoon measurements are level ones unless the recipe states otherwise.

Don't forget that all the ideas here are just to get you started. Have fun experimenting with your own creations when you're done with these.

You can even plan a "Gruesome Grub" cooking party with your friends for lots more foul fun!

3

Beheaded Alien

A perfect dessert that is easy to make and yummy to eat but looks really…gross!

What you will need:
- 2 boxes of lime Jell-O
- 6 marshmallows
- 6 pieces of dry spaghetti
- 2 licorice whirls or 2 candies
- measuring cup
- medium-size heatproof bowl
- plate

1 Use slightly less water to make firmer Jell-O.

Following the instructions on the boxes, make the Jell-O. Pour it into the bowl and put it in the refrigerator until set firm.

2 Dip the bowl in a sink of hot water for a few minutes to ease the Jell-O. Carefully turn it over onto a plate.

3 Push 3 marshmallows onto 3 pieces of spaghetti to create a tentacle. Repeat. Push into Jell-O. Position the eyes. Serve immediately.

Sick on Toast

A quick, easy, and very tasty snack. Just close your eyes while you eat it!

What you will need:

- 4 eggs
- ½ cup milk
- salt and pepper
- 1 tablespoon butter
- 1 tomato, diced
- 1 slice of ham, cut into small pieces
- 1 cooked carrot, diced
- 4 slices of toast
- bowl and wooden spoon
- nonstick saucepan

1

Break the eggs into the bowl. Add the milk and beat together. Add salt and pepper to taste.

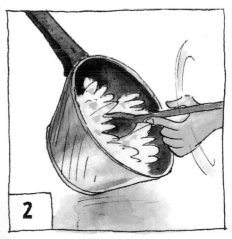

2

Melt the butter over medium heat and add the egg mixture. Stir until the mixture begins to solidify. Keep stirring!

3

When the mixture is firm, but not dry or burnt, remove it from the heat. Quickly stir in the tomato, ham, and carrot.

4

Spoon onto pieces of toast and eat immediately.

Disgusting Dips

Here are two gloppy mixtures you can dip into. You can dip carrots, sweet red and yellow peppers, bread sticks, cucumbers, or chips into the grunge.

Yuckamole

What you will need:
- 1 ripe avocado
- 2 heaping tablespoons cottage cheese
- 1–2 teaspoons lemon juice
- 1 tablespoon ketchup
- salt and pepper
- knife and fork
- bowl

1 Peel the avocado and mash it using a fork. Add all the other ingredients and stir.

2 Place in a bowl and serve immediately. If you leave it, it will gradually look yuckier and yuckier!

Cement

What you will need:
- 8 ounces cottage cheese with pineapple
- 2–3 tablespoons cream cheese
- 6 seedless green grapes, chopped into very small pieces
- 1$\frac{1}{2}$ teaspoons soy sauce
- some slices of toast
- bowl and spoon
- knife

1 Mix all the wet ingredients together in a bowl. To make the cement grayer, add more soy sauce.

2 Cut the toast into shovel shapes to serve with the cement.

Nasty Nibbles

These yucky lunchtime snacks can be made using muffins, buns, sliced bread, or toast—whatever you prefer.

Mouse Trap

Cut halfway through a muffin or soft bun. Stuff with shredded lettuce and place half of a hardboiled egg inside. Mix a little mayonnaise with ketchup and dribble over the "mouse." Add a piece of cooked spaghetti or a strip of cheese for the tail. Be careful as you bite into it!

stuffed olive slices for eyes

cucumber slices for scales

strips of red pepper to make fish lips

Fish Face

Drain a small can of tuna and mix with a little mayonnaise. Stir in some drained, canned sweet corn. Spoon on top of bread or toast and create your freaky fish face.

Egg Head

Make a tasty troll face using a topping of finely chopped hardboiled eggs and cucumber mixed with mayonnaise.

cucumber lips and sweet corn teeth

watercress hair

black olive eyes

red pepper or tomato nose

Blood and Guts

This is a really filling dinner dish with a deliciously gory sauce! Use a mixture of red, green, and white spaghetti, rigatoni, and fusilli for a great gutsy look.

Keep the lid on the saucepan.

1

Heat the oil in the medium saucepan and fry the onion and carrot until soft.

What you will need:
- 1 pound dry pasta, total
- 1 tablespoon olive or vegetable oil
- 1 medium onion, chopped
- 1 carrot, chopped very small or grated
- 14-ounce can chopped tomatoes
- pinch of mixed herbs
- salt and pepper
- 1 large and 1 medium saucepan (with lids)
- wooden spoon
- colander

2

Add the tomatoes, herbs, salt, and pepper. Stir, and let it simmer gently, uncovered, for about 20 minutes.

Cook until the pasta is soft but still has some "bite."

3

Fill the large pan with water. Add ½ teaspoon salt, bring it to a boil, and add the pasta. Cook for 10–12 minutes.

4

Strain the pasta. Toss it in the sauce before serving. (This makes it look gutsier!)

Throat Throttler

A sinister drink that Dracula would be proud of. It even has fangs to match. Try drinking while wearing them!

For each person you will need:
- 1 thick slice cucumber
- 1 glass cola
- 1 scoop ice cream (any flavor)
- knife
- tall glass
- 2 straws

1 First, cut out the fangs from the cucumber slice as shown. You can try them on, too!

2 Fill the glass halfway with cola. Add the ice cream and then top it off with more cola. Watch as it froths! Pop in the straws, decorate with the fangs, and serve.

For an extra scare, you can drop in a lychee nut or two before adding the ice cream. Use canned or fresh peeled ones. Just watch your friends' faces when they see what's lurking in their glasses.

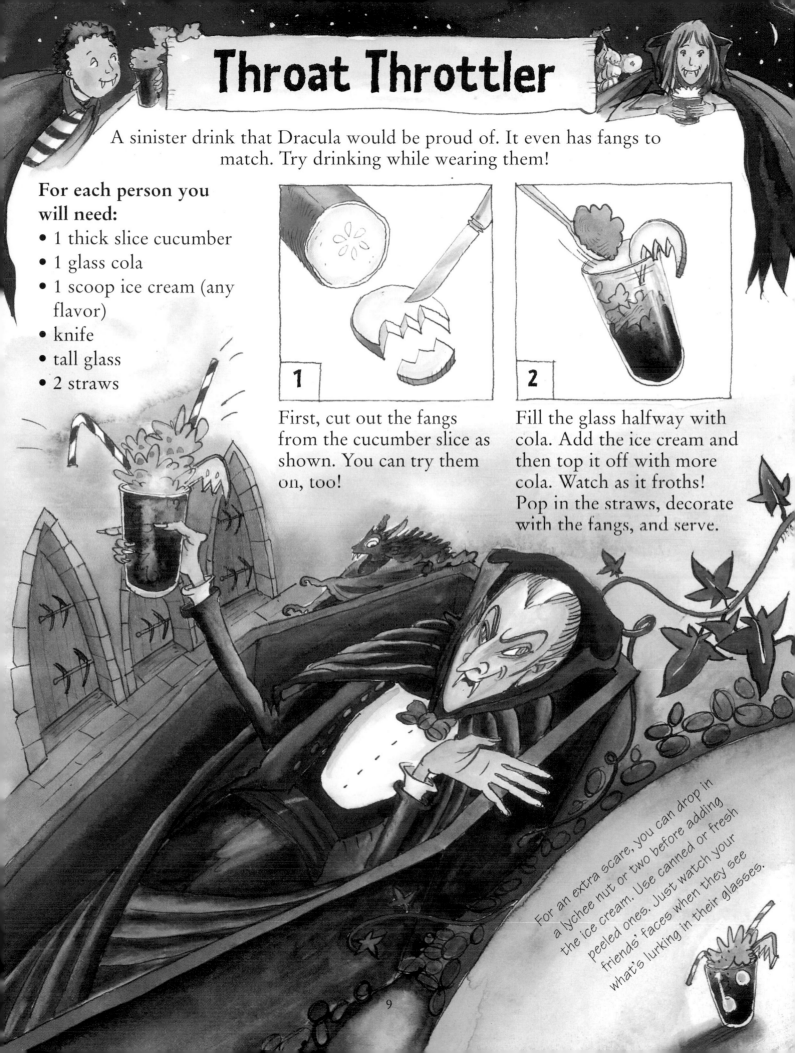

Creepy Cakes

These are perfect for Halloween parties, or any time you want to make your friends shudder. Use the basic cupcake recipe for all three variations.

Eyeball Cakes

What you will need to make 16–18 cupcakes:

- 1 stick softened butter or margarine
- ½ cup sugar
- 2 eggs
- ¾ cup self-rising flour
- ¾ cup powdered sugar, sifted
- 16–18 chocolate drops
- red food coloring
- bowl
- wooden and metal spoons
- 18 paper cupcake cups
- cupcake pan
- cooling rack
- butter knife
- small paintbrush (clean!)

1

In a bowl, cream the butter (or margarine) and sugar together until they are pale and fluffy.

2

Beat in the eggs, one at a time, adding a tablespoon of flour with each. Fold in the rest of the flour with a metal spoon.

3 Cool on the rack.

Put paper liners in cupcake pan. Spoon in equal amounts of mixture. Bake in the oven at 375°F for 15–20 minutes until risen and golden.

Mix the powdered sugar with 1 tablespoon or more hot water until smooth.

4

When cool, use the butter knife to cover the tops of cakes with icing. Put a chocolate drop in the center of each. Paint veins on the icing using the brush and red food coloring.

Bat Bites

Make chocolate cupcakes by substituting 1 tablespoon cocoa powder for 1 tablespoon flour.

Cut off tops of cupcakes, then cut the tops in half to make wings.

You will need a container of chocolate icing. Spoon a small blob on the center of each cupcake, position wings, and finish with silver balls for eyes.

Spider Sponges

Ice the cupcakes as on page 10 before decorating. You will need candy of different sizes and colors.

black candies for bodies

small candies for eyes

licorice strings for legs

Snail Buns

You will need licorice whirls, with or without colored centers.

Press licorice whirl down on top of a thick layer of white icing. Don't worry if your snails don't hold their heads up very high!

Cut a slit down a licorice whirl to make snail antlers.

11

Munch a Monster

A tasty treat to give your family and friends a real scare. If you don't want to make the pizza dough, you can buy ready-made individual-size pizza crusts at the supermarket.

What you will need to make 4 small monsters:

- 1¼ cups all-purpose flour
- 2 teaspoons yeast
- 1 teaspoon salt
- ½ cup warm water
- 14-ounce can chopped tomatoes, drained
- 1 tablespoon tomato purée
- salt and pepper

- pinch of mixed herbs
- 1 large and 1 small bowl
- wooden spoon
- plastic bag, dusted inside with flour
- rolling pin
- well-greased baking tray

1

Mix the flour, yeast, and salt in the large bowl. Add the water and mix to a soft dough.

2

Knead the dough with floured hands for a few minutes. Put it in the bag and leave in a warm place for 15–20 minutes.

3

Dust work surface with flour.

Mix the tomatoes with the tomato purée, salt, pepper, and herbs. Divide the dough into 4 balls. Roll or press each one out into a circle about 6 inches across.

4

Place the circles on the baking tray and spread tomato sauce on each one. Add your toppings before baking at 400°F for 20–25 minutes.

Let your imagination run away with you and create some really monstrous toppings. Sweet corn kernels make great teeth. Layers of sliced zucchini, pepperoni, and stuffed olives make ghastly eyes. Use a slice of mushroom for a nose, and make hideous hair out of yellow, red, and green peppers.

Try cutting the dough into other awful shapes—like skulls!

Snot Surfers

A tasty bowl of slime topped with brave surfers.
Eat them quickly before they fall into the gunky depths!

What you will need:
- 1 medium onion
- 3 medium leeks, thoroughly washed
- 1 large potato, peeled
- 1 tablespoon butter
- 4 cups chicken or vegetable stock
- salt and pepper
- 4 slices of toast
- knife
- large saucepan with lid
- wooden spoon
- strainer or blender and bowl
- gingerbread man cutter

Stir occasionally.

1

Thinly slice the onion, leeks, and potato. Cook gently in the butter for 10 minutes. Keep the lid on.

2

Add the stock, salt, and pepper. Simmer for about 15 minutes. Then strain or liquefy in a blender.

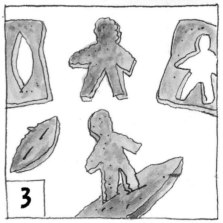

3

Cut out your toast surfers and their surfboards. Make slits in the boards and insert the surfers' feet. Serve one surfer on each bowl of soup.

Slushy Slurps

Use as many different flavored juices as you like to make these poisonous-looking—but definitely delicious—drinks.

What you will need:
- fruit juices of your choice
- ice cube trays
- strong plastic bags and ties
- rolling pin
- glasses and straws

grape

pineapple

lime

orange lemon apple

1

2

3

Pour the juices into ice cube trays. Put them in the freezer for a few hours or overnight.

When frozen, pop the ice cubes out, one color at a time, into a plastic bag. Seal the bag and smash the cubes with the rolling pin to crush them well.

Layer the colors as vividly as you like in glasses. Sip through a straw.

Dead Man's Hand

A gruesome centerpiece for any party table, this will really revolt your friends and family. You need to put it in the refrigerator to defrost slightly before serving—just until the fingers wiggle!

What you will need:

- 1 new large rubber glove, washed very well
- 1 box of hardened lemon or orange Jell-O
- 1 box of hardened red Jell-O
- red food coloring
- red licorice strings
- measuring cup
- pitcher and spoon
- 3 clothespins
- large plate
- scissors
- small paintbrush (clean!)

Make sure the Jell-O is well dissolved in the hot water.

1 Break the Jell-O into pieces. Place in the pitcher and dissolve in 1⅓ cups boiling water. Then add 1⅓ cups cold water.

2 You really need two people for this.

Over a sink, pour the mixture into the glove and seal it well by folding over the opening at least twice and pinning it firmly.

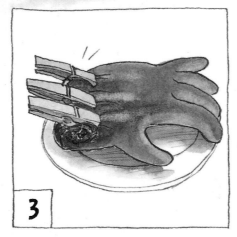

3 Place the hand palm-side-down on a plate. Space out the fingers. Put it in the freezer overnight.

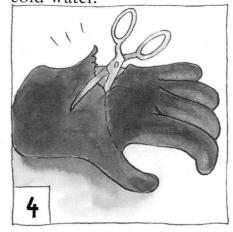

4 Cut the glove, bit by bit, and gradually peel it off the Jell-O.

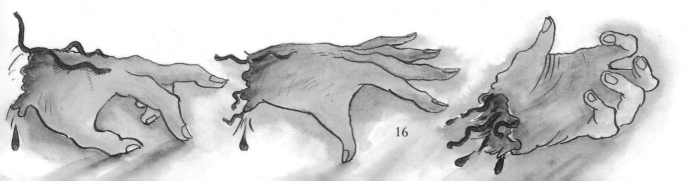

Decorating the hand:

Brush on the red food coloring to make it look as gory as possible. Don't forget the stump as well as the nails!

As the hand defrosts, the coloring will run a bit—this will make it look even creepier.

Place red licorice strings on the back of the hand for veins.

If you eat one finger first, you can really freak out your friends!

17

Yeti Foot

A great gory foot that makes you glad the rest of the creature isn't around. Serve it with some salad or other vegetables for a complete monster meal!

What you will need:

- 4–5 medium potatoes, peeled, cut into chunks
- 1 tablespoon butter
- ⅓ cup all-purpose flour
- 1 egg, beaten
- 4 ounces cheddar cheese, grated
- salt and pepper
- ketchup
- large saucepan
- potato masher
- wooden spoon
- greased baking tray

1

Sculpt and mold into shape.

2

3

Cook the potatoes in a pan of water until soft (about 15–20 minutes). Drain them, and stir in the butter. Mash until smooth.

Mix in the flour, egg, and cheese. Season to taste. Place the mixture on the baking tray and sculpt in the shape of a foot with three toes.

Bake in the oven at 425°F for 15 minutes or until golden brown. Serve with the ketchup dribbled on top of it.

Bony Cookies

These skull and bone cookies are great fun to make. You can use red licorice strings to tie some bones together. Don't worry if your shapes look a bit rough around the edges—they may have been buried for some time!

What you will need to make 18–20 cookies:

- 1¼ cups all-purpose flour
- ⅓ cup sugar
- 6 tablespoons butter
- grated lemon rind (optional)
- 1 small egg, beaten
- a few raisins
- bowl and wooden spoon
- rolling pin
- knife
- greased baking sheet
- cooling rack

1 Use only your fingertips and thumbs.

2

3 Push in raisins to make nostrils.

Mix the flour and sugar in the bowl. Work in the butter until it is like fine bread crumbs.

Add the lemon rind, if using, and enough egg to mix to a stiff dough.

Roll out on a floured surface and cut out your skulls and bones. Place on baking sheets and bake in the oven at 350°F for 10–15 minutes. Cool on a rack.

Maggot Cocktail

Invite your friends to try this squirmy starter—it really is delicious. It looks its wriggliest in glass dishes.

What you will need:
- ½ pound cooked, peeled shrimp (defrosted if frozen)
- 4 tablespoons mayonnaise
- 2 teaspoons ketchup
- 2 teaspoons lemon juice
- pepper
- shredded lettuce leaves
- lemon slices
- spoon
- bowl
- 4 dishes
- greased baking sheet

1

Mix together the mayonnaise, ketchup, and lemon juice. Add pepper to taste. Leave aside about 16 prawns and stir the rest into the mixture.

2

You don't need to be too neat!

Make a bed of lettuce in each dish and spoon some shrimp mixture on top.

3

Serve with whole-grain bread.

Garnish with the lemon slices and remaining shrimp. Make them look like escaping maggots! Keep in the refrigerator until ready to serve.

Stinky Puffs

These look great as they puff up, but when you bite into them...phew! What a stink!

What you will need to make 8 puffs:

- 17½-ounce package ready-made puff pastry (defrosted if frozen)
- 1½ ounces gorgonzola cheese
- 1 egg, beaten
- flour for dusting
- rolling pin
- 3-inch round pastry cutter
- pastry brush
- baking sheet
- knife

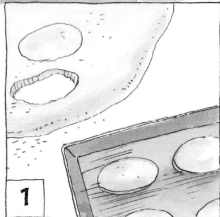

1

On a floured surface, roll out the pastry until it is ¼-inch thick. Cut out 16 rounds. Place 8 on the baking sheet.

2

Put a piece of cheese in the middle of each. Brush the pastry edges with egg. Place the remaining rounds on top. Press down and pinch the edges firmly.

3

Cut a small slit in each top. Brush on some more egg and bake in the oven at 425°F for 10–15 minutes. Serve hot.

Cowpat Pudding

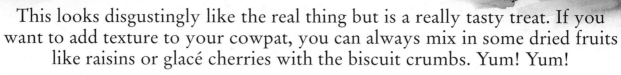

This looks disgustingly like the real thing but is a really tasty treat. If you want to add texture to your cowpat, you can always mix in some dried fruits like raisins or glacé cherries with the biscuit crumbs. Yum! Yum!

What you will need:

- 8-ounce package wholemeal tea biscuits
- 1 stick butter, cut into pieces
- 4 ounces plain chocolate, broken into pieces
- green licorice strings
- a few raisins
- large plastic bag and tie
- rolling pin
- mixing bowl
- 8-inch round cake pan
- aluminum foil
- small saucepan
- wooden spoon

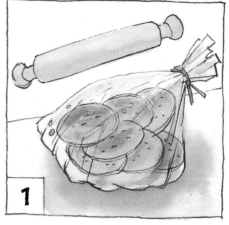

1

Put the biscuits in the bag. Seal it. Crush into tiny crumbs with the rolling pin. Empty into the bowl.

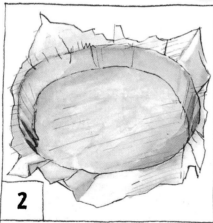

2

Line the pan with foil, making sure it goes right into the edges.

Make sure all crumbs are coated.

3

Put the butter and chocolate in the saucepan and heat gently. Stir until the chocolate is melted. Pour into the biscuit mix.

4

Spoon the mixture into the pan. Press it down and use the back of the spoon to make circular patterns on top. Refrigerate for at least 2 hours.

To decorate your cowpat:

On a large plate, arrange clumps of green licorice strings. Lift the cowpat out of its pan and remove the foil.

Instead of licorice strings, you can use a green plate or dish as "grass."

Place the cowpat on the "grass" and decorate with a few raisin "flies" or "dung beetles."

Axeman's Snacks

Ideal party food for a ghoulish occasion—these are simple to make and look really horrible. Don't leave them where someone fainthearted might find them.

What you will need:

- 4 hot dogs
- 8 small sandwich rolls
- 1 radish
- ketchup
- wooden spoon
- knife

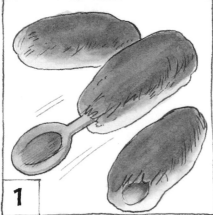

1 Use the handle of the spoon to push a hole almost all the way through each roll.

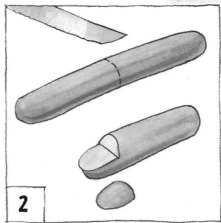

2 Spoon a little ketchup into each hole. Cut each hot dog in half, then cut a "bed" for each nail in each closed end.

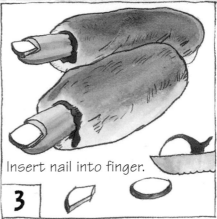

Insert nail into finger.

3 Push half a hot dog into each roll. Cut a thin slice of radish, and then a wedge from this. Trim to make a nail.

24